4/00

6D -04 -07 -82
72 -ALL -497

MONSTER JOKES

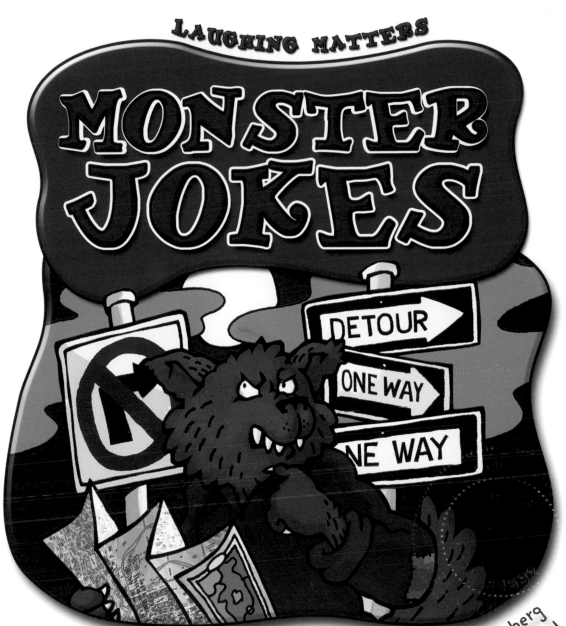

Compiled by Pam Rosenberg
Illustrated by Patrick Girouard

Special thanks to Donna Hynek and her second grade class of 2005–2006 for sharing their favorite jokes.

Published in the United States of America by The Child's World®
PO Box 326, Chanhassen, MN 55317-0326
800-599-READ
www.childsworld.com

Acknowledgments
    The Child's World®: Mary Berendes, Publishing Director

    Editorial Directions, Inc.: E. Russell Primm, Editorial Director and Line Editor; Katie Marsico, Managing Editor; Assistant Editor, Caroline Wood; Susan Ashley, Proofreader

    The Design Lab: Kathleen Petelinsek, Designer; Kari Tobin, Page Production

Library of Congress Cataloging-in-Publication Data
    Monster jokes / compiled by Pam Rosenberg;
    illustrated by Patrick Girouard.
        p. cm. — (Laughing matters)
    ISBN-13 978-1-59296-707-0
    ISBN-10 1-59296-707-8 (library bound : alk. paper)
    I. Monsters—Juvenile humor. I. Rosenberg, Pam. II. Girouard, Patrick.
III. Title. IV. Series.
    PN6231.M665M64 2007
    818'.60208037—dc22   2006022653

MONSTER JOKES

Why couldn't the mummy
answer the phone?
He was tied up.

3

Why don't mummies take vacations?
They're afraid they will relax and unwind.

Where do mummies go for a swim?
The Dead Sea.

How can you tell if a mummy has a cold?
He starts coffin.

How did the mummy react to the dull class?
It was bored stiff.

Why was the mummy sent into the game as a pinch hitter?
Because the game was all tied up.

What did the scientist get when he crossed a mummy and a stopwatch?
An old-timer.

VAMPIRES

Why doesn't the vampire have a lot of friends?
Because he's a pain in the neck.

What's a vampire's favorite holiday?
Fangsgiving Day.

What dogs are the best pets for vampires?
Bloodhounds.

How does a vampire like his food served?
In bite-size pieces.

What would you get if you crossed Count Dracula and Jesse James?
A robbery at the blood bank.

How would a vampire like to see a horse race finish?
Neck and neck.

What's a vampire's favorite fruit?
A neck-tarine.

Pete: What would you get if you crossed a vampire and a camp counselor?
Dan: I don't know, but I wouldn't want to be in his cabin!

What do vampires take at eleven o'clock every day?
A coffin break.

Why did the vampire want to go to biology class?
He heard the teacher was an old bat.

Which vampire ate the three bears' porridge?
Ghouldilocks.

What do you get when you cross a teacher with a vampire?
Lots of blood tests.

7

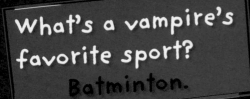

What is Dracula's favorite landmark?
The Vampire State Building.

What's the difference between a baseball player and a vampire?
One bats flies and the other flies bats.

How do you join the Dracula fan club?
You send in your name, address, and blood type.

Why aren't vampires welcome at the blood bank?
Because they only want to make withdrawals.

SKELETONS

What happened to the ship that sank in the sea filled with piranhas?
It came back with a skeleton crew.

What do you call a skeleton who won't get up in the morning?
Lazy bones.

Who won the skeleton beauty contest?
No body.

Why didn't the skeleton dance at the party?
She had no body to dance with.

Why don't skeletons play music in church?
They have no organs.

Who was the most famous French skeleton?
Napoléon Bone-apart.

Why don't skeletons play football?
Because they can't make body contact.

What kind of plate does a skeleton eat off of?
Bone china.

Why do skeletons hate winter?
Because the wind goes right through them.

Why wouldn't the skeleton jump off the diving board?
It had no guts.

What do you call a skeleton who presses a doorbell?
A dead ringer.

What do you get if you cross a bunch of bones and a week in Florida?
A skele-tan.

What's a skeleton's favorite musical instrument?
A trom-bone.

WITCHES

What do you call a witch's garage? A broom closet.

Why do witches ride on broomsticks? Because vacuum cleaners are too heavy.

13

Why don't angry witches ride their broomsticks?
They're afraid they'll fly off the handle.

What do witches put in their hair?
Scare spray.

How do witches travel when they don't have a broom?
They witch-hike.

What is a witch's favorite subject in school?
Spelling.

Why did the witch keep turning into Mickey Mouse?
She kept having Disney spells.

What noise does a witch's breakfast cereal make?
Snap, cackle, pop!

What do baby witches play with?
Deady bears.

What happens when you see twin witches?
It's not easy to tell which witch is which!

What do you get if you cross a dinosaur and a witch?
Tyrannosaurus hex.

Who flies on a broom and carries a medicine bag?
A witch doctor.

What do you get if you cross a witch and an iceberg?
A cold spell.

Why do witches wear pointy hats?
To keep their heads warm.

How did the witch feel after she was run over by a car?
Tired.

What do you call a witch with poison ivy?
An itchy witchy.

What has six legs and flies?
A witch giving her black cat a ride.

15

MONSTER TONGUE TWISTERS

Peggy Babcock's mummy,
Peggy Babcock's mummy,
Peggy Babcock's mummy.

Mummies munch much mush;
Monsters munch much mush;
Many mummies and monsters
Must munch much mush.

The wretched witch watched a walrus washing.
Did the wretched witch watch a walrus washing?
If the wretched witch watched a walrus washing,
Where's the washing walrus the wretched witch
    watched?

If two witches watched two watches,
which witch would watch which watch?

GHOSTS & GHOULS

Why did the ghost go to the carnival?
It wanted to go on the rollerghoster.

What kind of street does a ghost like best?
A dead end.

What position did the monster play on the hockey team?
Ghoulie.

17

Where do ghosts get an education? High sghouls.

What airline do ghouls fly? British Scareways.

What kind of jewels do ghosts wear? Tombstones.

Where do ghosts go on vacation? Lake Eerie.

What do ghosts eat for dinner? Ghoulash.

Why are graveyards so noisy? Because of all the coffins.

What do you call a prehistoric ghost? A terror-dactyl.

What did the baby ghost eat for lunch? A boo-loney sandwich.

What trees do ghouls like best? Ceme-trees.

What kind of music do ghosts dance to?

Soul music.

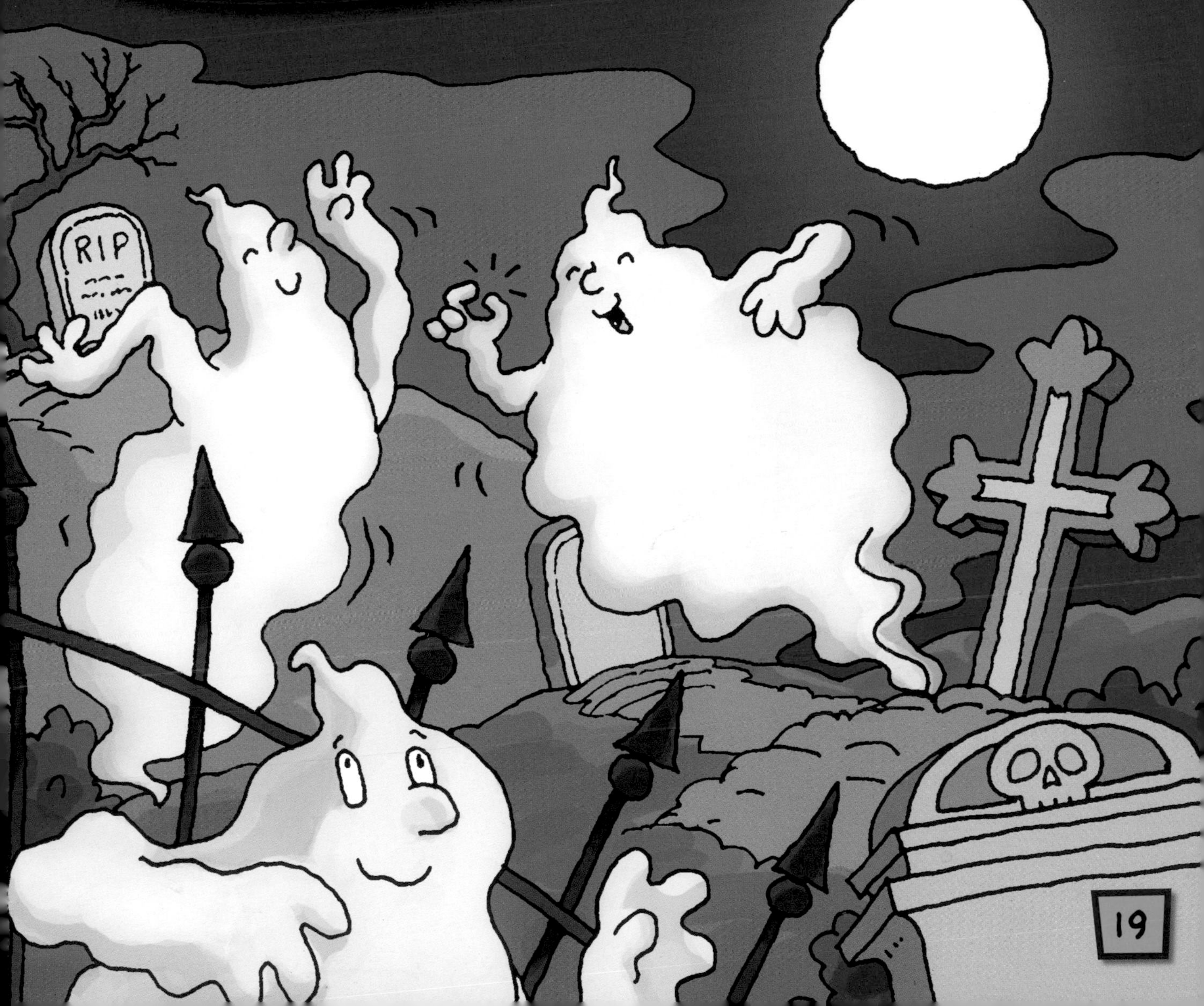

MISCELLANEOUS MONSTER JOKES

What's a monster's favorite soup?
Scream of tomato.

AAAAAAAAHHH

What do you call a monster that chases a whole football team?
Hungry!

What inning is it when the Frankenstein monster is up to bat?
The fright-inning.

What happens if you upset a cannibal?
You get into hot water!

Where do zombies go on vacation?
Club Dead.

What do demons have on vacation?
A devil of a time.

What do you call a hairy beast with clothes on?
A wear-wolf.

Where does the werewolf sit at the movies?
Anywhere he wants to.

What do you call a hairy beast that's lost?
A where-wolf.

Knock knock.
Who's there?
Voodoo.
Voodoo who?
Voodoo you think you are?

Knock knock.
Who's there?
Zombies.
Zombies who?
Zombies make honey, and zombies don't.

What do black cats eat for breakfast?
Mice krispies.

What do demons eat for breakfast?
Deviled eggs.

Why was the werewolf arrested at the butcher shop?
He was caught chop lifting.

Girl Monster: Mommy, my teacher said I was neat, pretty, and well-behaved.
Mommy Monster: Don't worry, dear, you'll do better next time!

What did the cannibal order when he went to a restaurant?
A waiter.

What happened at the cannibals' wedding party?
They toasted the bride and groom.

What does a cannibal call a skateboarder?
Meals on wheels.

What did the cannibal say when he was full?
I couldn't eat another mortal!

How can you help a starving cannibal?
Give him a hand.

About Patrick Girouard:

Patrick Girouard has been illustrating books for almost 15 years but still looks remarkably lifelike. He loves reading, movies, coffee, robots, a beautiful red-haired lady named Rita, and especially his sons, Marc and Max. Here's an interesting fact: A dog named Sam lives under his drawing board. You can visit him (Patrick, not Sam) at www.pgirouard.com.

About Pam Rosenberg:

Pam Rosenberg is a former junior high school teacher and corporate trainer. She currently works as an author, editor, and the mother of Sarah and Jake. She took on this project as a service to all her fellow parents of young children. At least now their kids will have lots of jokes to choose from when looking for the one they will tell their parents over and over and over again!